CATS

OF THE
ISLE OF WIGHT

British Library Cataloguing
in Publication Data

A catalogue record for this book is
available from the British Library

CATS
OF THE
ISLE OF WIGHT

Verses and photographs
by
Billie Love

Their Homes
Their Lives
Their Fun and Folly

By the same author

'Opusses'
'How to become a child'
'Sheba and the White Whisker'

Published in Great Britain by
The Billie Love Historical Collection
Reflections, Winton Street, Ryde
Isle of Wight PO33 2BX

© Billie Love 2003
Second edition, 2009
Third edition, 2012

Designed and printed by Crossprint 01983 524885

ISBN 978-0-9518410-4-4

With thanks to Anna Shepherd for her encouragement and for her picture of 'Luke through the window' on page 54

CONTENTS

		Page
Daisy		2
Chilly Billy		4
Shanty		6
Pernickety Pet		8
Coxcomb		10
Crescendo		12
Cleo		14
Scattergood		16
Major Difficulties		18
Sophie Paws		20
Wight Watchman		22
Cat Burglar		24
Lonely		26
Collared		28
Up-Market		30
Down-Market		32
Jake awake		34
Troy Boy		36
Rebel		38
Starlet		40
Picked and Nicked		42
Coastguard		44
Parishioners		46
Daredevil		48
Uptails All		50
Upstairs cat		52
Cat Sitter		54
A Weighty Problem		56
Uproar		58
Lap-cat		60
Manx		62
Claws and Effect		64
Senior Citizen		66
Adgestone Dreamer		68

Daisy

I've had so many kittens
And they've all gone far and wide
To Colwell Bay and Freshwater
To Shanklin, Brook and Ryde

I've got a boy at Sutton
Achieving great success
He digs up bones of dinosaurs
He does get in a mess

The twins were sent to Osborne
To keep the mice at bay
They've gone a bit superior
While chasing royal prey

My youngest is at Shalfleet
His life's a risky slog
He needs a cat's diplomacy
He's living with a dog.

I've a little girl in Brighstone
Who's in the family way
She's hoping that her progeny
Will outnumber mine one day

I feel I've done my duty
With kids in every place
You could say that my family
Is the Round the Island Race.

CHILLY BILLY

Chilly Billy's what they call him
Chilly Billy feels the cold
Little Billy was abandoned
When he wasn't very old

Kindly folk discovered Billy
Picked him up and rescued him
Soaking wet and so bedraggled
Thought his chances very slim

Lots of love and lots of fussing
Soon got Billy on his feet
Godshill folk are quite warm-hearted
Billy's pleasure is complete

Billy knows there are some places
Where he's not supposed to go
He's heat-seeking for his comfort
Takes a chance they will not know

Where to find him, that's the problem
Like a disappearing elf
All curled up beneath the bedclothes
Or the airing cupboard shelf

Strange to say that though he's coddled
Safe behind those sheltering doors
Warmed by every kind of heating
Billy always has cold paws.

SHANTY

Ship ahoy!
lt's the Bembridge boy
A sailor cat
That you would employ
When planning a trip
To the China seas
Or the arctic wastes
Or antipodes

We know that cats
Help to fight the rats
They do the job
With valour, and that's
What the Captain wants
The rewards are great
A catnip mouse
And a loaded plate

He'll toss his tail
At a storm or gale
With his courage all set
For a world-wide sail
But he won't get far
On the roaring foam
He's a land-locked Tar
In a house-boat home.

PERNICKETY PET

Stroppy from Carisbrooke's hard to please
Nutrition is tough to maintain
The numerous packets and pouches and tins
He'll regard with distaste and disdain

Stroppy's fond owner spends hours at the shops
Examining well-displayed shelves
Decisions, decisions you hear her sad cry
I wish they would shop for themselves

Fishypal, Meaticat, Cattitins, Yums,
Pussygrub – every daft name
"I wonder," she says, "what the recipes are
I'll bet, underneath, they're the same"

Stroppy's fond carer does all that she can
The worry is making her thinner
We think the real reason is all Stroppy's fault
When all that he'll eat is her dinner.

Coxcomb

Basil of Freshwater's terribly vain
At least that is what you would think
He can't pass a mirror without a proud glance
Where he'll pose with a nod and a wink

We've noticed, by puddles and small local streams
He will pause and bend, so he can see
His handsome reflection and all his best points
Then walk on with renewed jeu d'esprit

We acknowledge his ears are superb and upright
His whiskers are long, we agree
We notice his fur is quite shiny and bright
We know that he's chic – so does he

He spends so much time on his washing routine
For perfection he tries to attain
That if someone strokes him or tickles his chin
He's obliged to start over again

We think that he's noticed photographers near
Inspired by that Dimbola Dame
Maybe he's hoping his likeness is caught
Achieving perpetual fame.

CRESCENDO

Oliver is his name
The same
As Dickens' delicate lad
Oliver too is small, but glad
To have affection
And a family connection
But where he's not little by choice
He makes up for it in voice
His imperative "meow"
Is a deafening row
That echoes up the lane
Down Shanklin Chine and back again
Even his purr is like
The revving of a motor-bike
We try to keep him quiet
With an almost non-stop diet
But if Oliver wants some more
He'll roar.
Neighbours do protest
And we just can't keep a guest
Mew and meow and purr and yell –
How do you make a padded cell?

CLEO

She was sad she was thin
When we first took her in
She deserved all our love and affection
We knew that she'd wish
For a portion of fish
And every good dish you could mention
To add to her joys
We bought her some toys
In colours unreal and exotic
We found we had erred
Because she preferred
Antics absurd and chaotic
She would scramble about
With her ears inside out
And chase every shadow she noticed
She'd give us a start
When she'd suddenly dart
Through my kitchen
Ignoring my protest
She will jump, she will leap
And land in a heap
Some shadow that moves is enthralling
But if there's no sun
No shadow, no fun
Then she's glum and her temper's appalling.

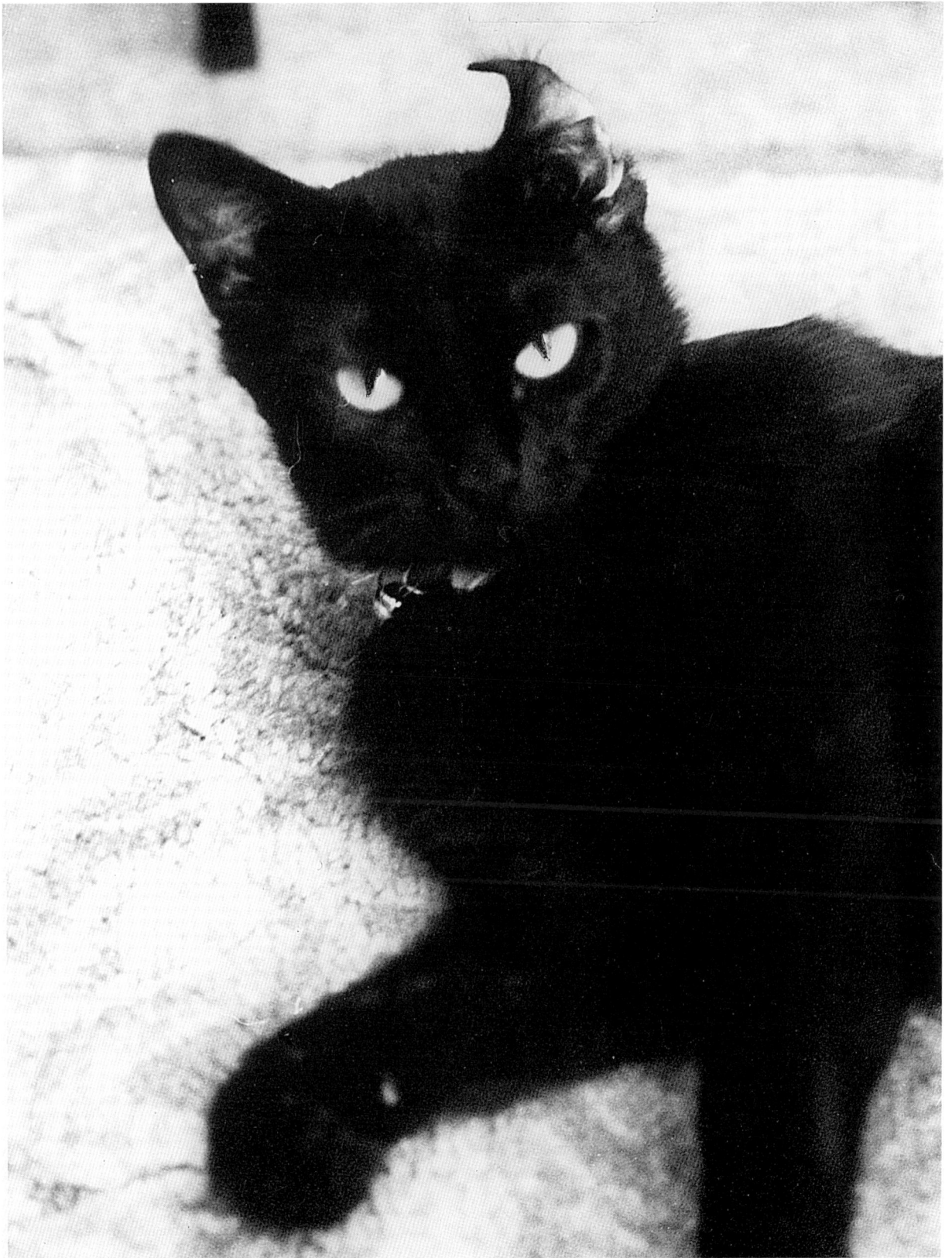

SCATTERGOOD

Scattergood's a lovely cat
Says local Mrs. Wright
Don't know where he gets to
For he's always out all night
He comes in every morning
For the breakfast I supply
But even if it's rained all night
He wanders in bone dry

My cat Scat is lovely
Says neighbour Mrs, Bright
He goes off every morning
But he's on my bed each night
I don't know where he gets to
But he's certainly well-fed
I always give him biscuits
Before we go to bed

Says little schoolgirl Sarah
"I love my Scatty so
He comes to greet me after school
But soon he wants to go
My Mum says he's a wanderer
And hardly ever stays
I hope to keep him near me
In the summer holidays"

So Sarah and the ladies
And maybe others too
Keep Scattergood alert and keen
He's lots of things to do
For he's on hand to cheer them up
If anyone gets low
Affection and a friendly purr
For the folks he likes to know.

MAJOR DIFFICULTIES

Maja lives in Ventnor
And is always in a hurry
Indeed he rushes round so fast
He really is a worry
He tears along the passage
He wants to go out – but
He just can't stop before he sees
The front door's firmly shut

Maja's headlong rushes
Sometimes end up in disaster
He's often been restricted
With his tail wrapped round in plaster
We know he once rushed up a tree
And stayed up there all night
It isn't true that when cats fall
They always land upright

We all assumed that dignity
Was natural to a feline
If Maja thinks it's dinner-time
He makes a frantic bee-line
He tears into the kitchen
To the corner where he's fed
He runs so fast he ends up
With his dish upon his head

He's known around the district
As the fastest cat in town
He'll take a chance on high-jump
And complete it upside down
His speed is such that local kids
Will often make a wager
That he's faster than a whippet
Yelling "Here's the galloping Maja"

Sophie Paws

This pretty cat lives in St. Helens
Her name is Sophie Paws,
In winter she likes to live by the hearth
In summer she stays outdoors.

The first home she had she abandoned quite soon,
As she fell for a Siamese
They both ran away and lived in a barn
In a life wild and free as the breeze.

She got bored with this life and the limited food
She eloped with a different Tom
But then she regretted the comfort she'd lost
At the very first home she'd come from

It really is scandalous, shocking to some
The way that she has behaved
The local cats gossip about her past sins
For they think she was almost depraved.

But now at St. Helens she's finally settled
She has learned her lesson at last
We think she's enjoying her leisurely life
And hope she can live down her past.

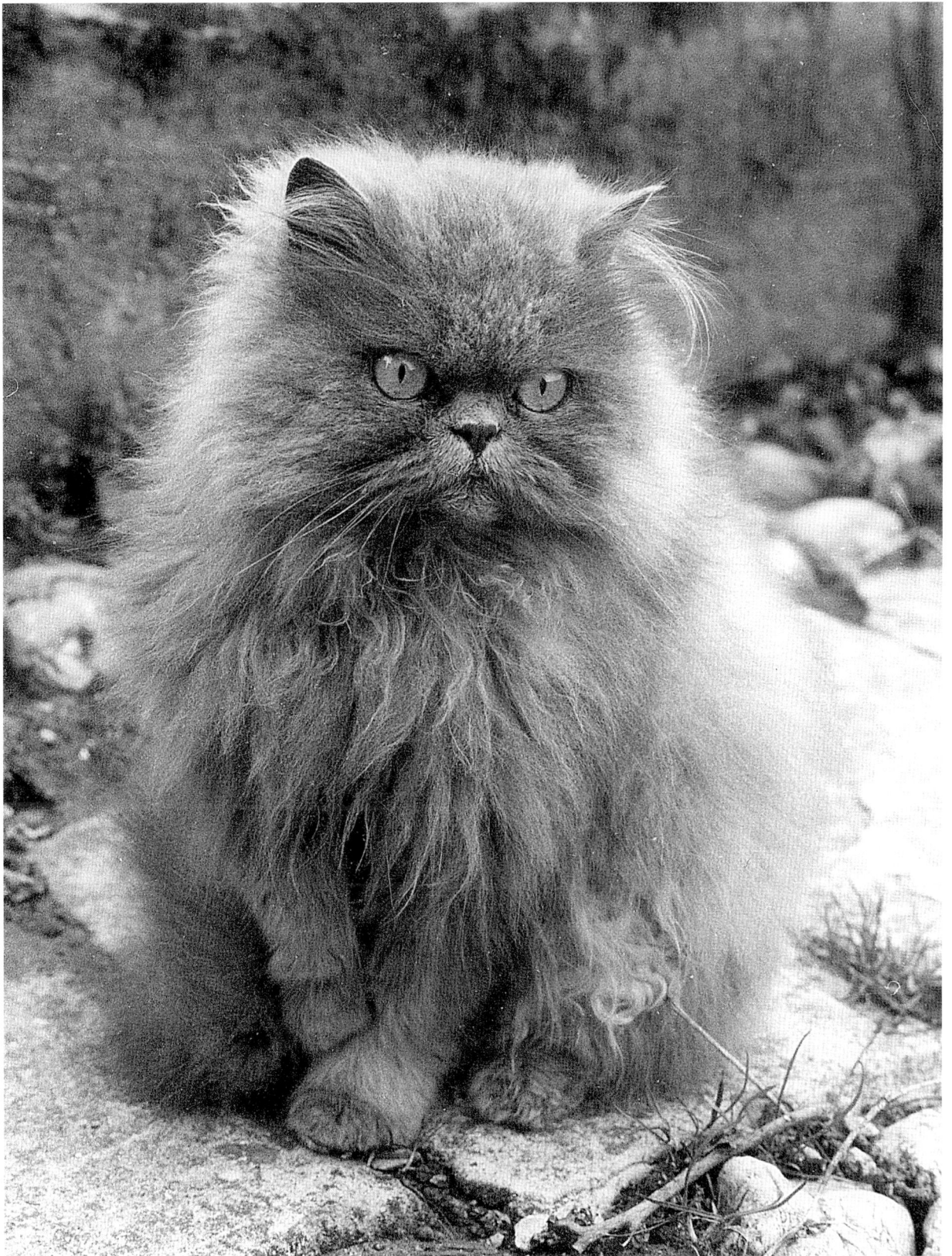

WIGHT WATCHMAN

When the dusk begins to fall
The Wight night-watchman
Starts his round
His hearing so acute
And so aware of every sound
A mouse late home
Will, frantic, scurry
Jabez watches
Doesn't hurry
To start some scrambling chase
Dignity will not permit
Such juvenile antics
For such a harum scarum small titbit
Every night he wanders
Seen by those returning late
What, one wonders is he seeking
Maybe some seductive mate?
There is a strangeness
In his eyes so bright
He seems to contemplate
The stars soft light
Like some moon-god's acolyte.
When comes the dawn
He'll turn and look
Towards his loving home at Brook

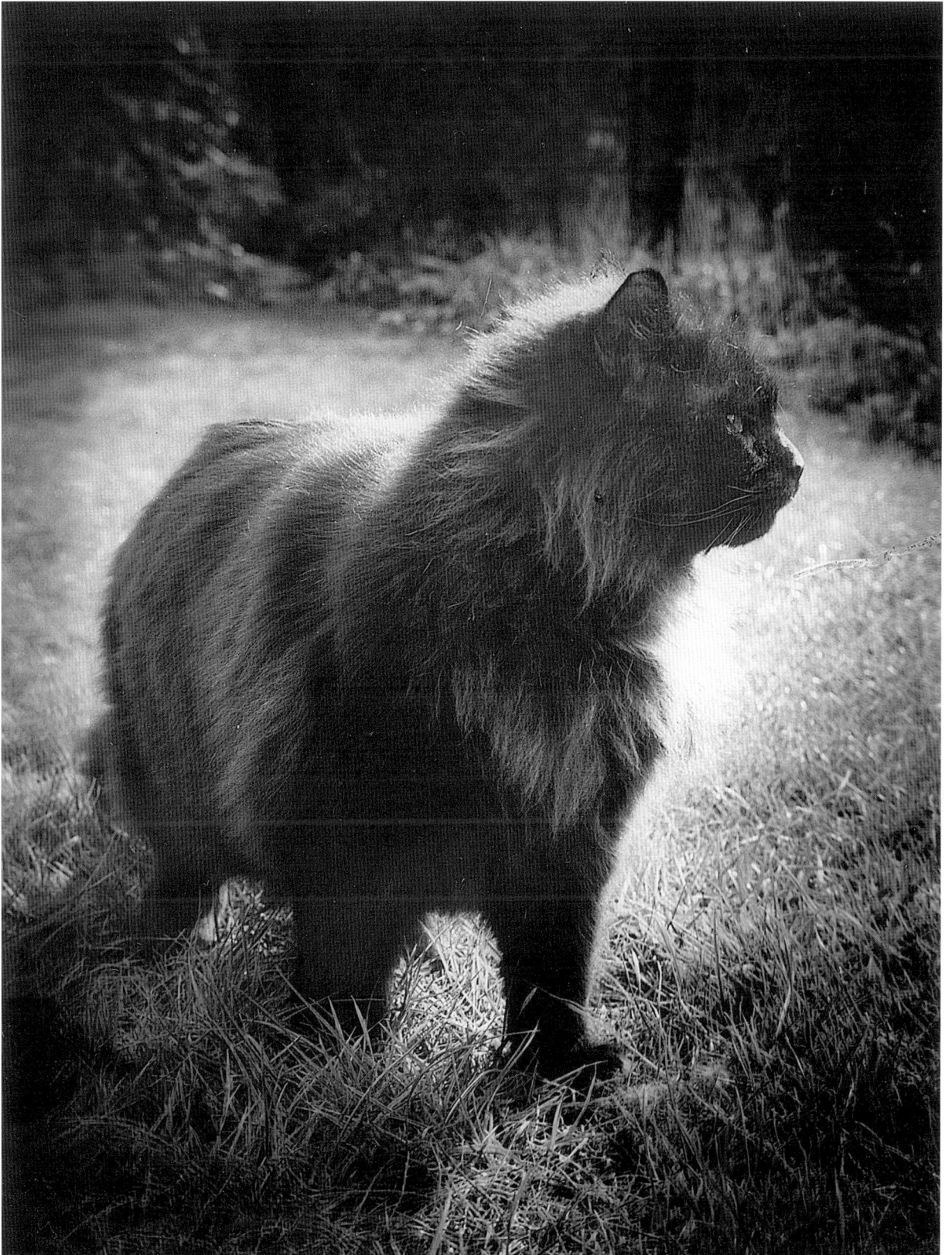

CAT BURGLAR

He started his life as Cuddles of Cowes
But we soon realised it was not the right name
He might achieve fame
If we re-named him Raffles
Or perhaps Sherlock Holmes
For he'd go on a foray to neighbouring homes
To detect where the tastiest titbits are hidden
Unbidden
He'll slip through a door left ajar and he'll raid
An elegant table that's beautifully laid
For people – not cats
But because he is one of the best acrobats
He will quietly abscond
And is quickly beyond
Detection
Complete with a savoury confection
Which he'll happily devour
In the following hour
He's not learned a lot from apparent success
He once went to burgle a different address
And you don't disregard a
Self-locking larder
He was there for many a day
For the people had just gone away
He was shocked
But relieved that the place was well-stocked
And when they returned to the flat
He was scared, he was home-sick – and fat
He's now back at home
And unlikely to roam
For he always remembers the time
When <u>he</u> was a victim of crime.

LONELY

The people that I live with
Are always going out
I hear them say "I won't be long"
But this is what I doubt
For I'm waiting in the hall
Where I hope to hear them call
But it's usually very late
Before I hear the garden gate
And I've been very lonely
And the food they've left is only
Biscuits and my water bowl
You know that really can't console
Arreton is very nice
But all I've got for chums are mice
Sympathy is what I need
I know I'll have a lovely feed
When they come home and fuss and pet me
Unaware they have upset me
But just when I have settled
And my humour I regain
They all get up and chatter
Then they all go out again

COLLARED

I'm not allowed out
I can tell you, I shout
I mew and I wail
And I lash with my tail
They stroke me and cuddle me but
The door remains shut
At Newport my doctors were kind
So surely they wouldn't mind
If I walked in the garden
I think that they'd pardon
A leap on the fence
I've got enough sense
Not to wander too far
With things as they are
For I've got this ridiculous collar
Though I holler
And growl and I cough
They won't take it off.
It seems I was ill with my ear
Oh dear
The things I've endured
But I think that I'm cured
Though a ramble would be a bit tricky
My friends might all take the micky.

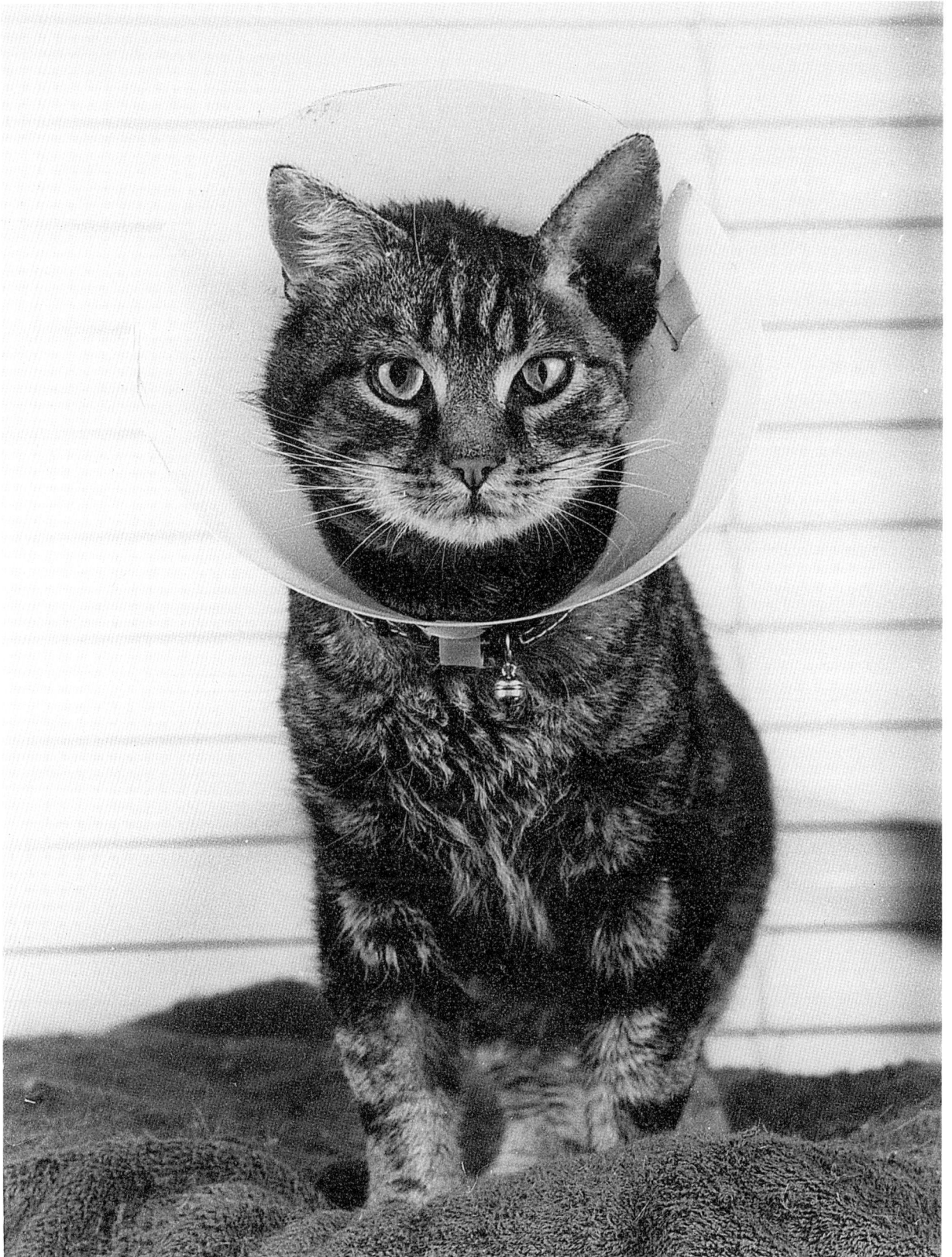

Up-market

Could you ever have a land
As beautiful as Yaverland?
The country is so spacious
And their Manor House is gracious
No wonder that their cats have sense
And give respect to residents.
Whether they're by cosy hearth
Or lounging on the garden path
The cats feel quite superior
To Inferior
Cats down-town
In nearby Sandown
Yaverland cats are the cream
And society's dream
And they love it –
The cream I mean.

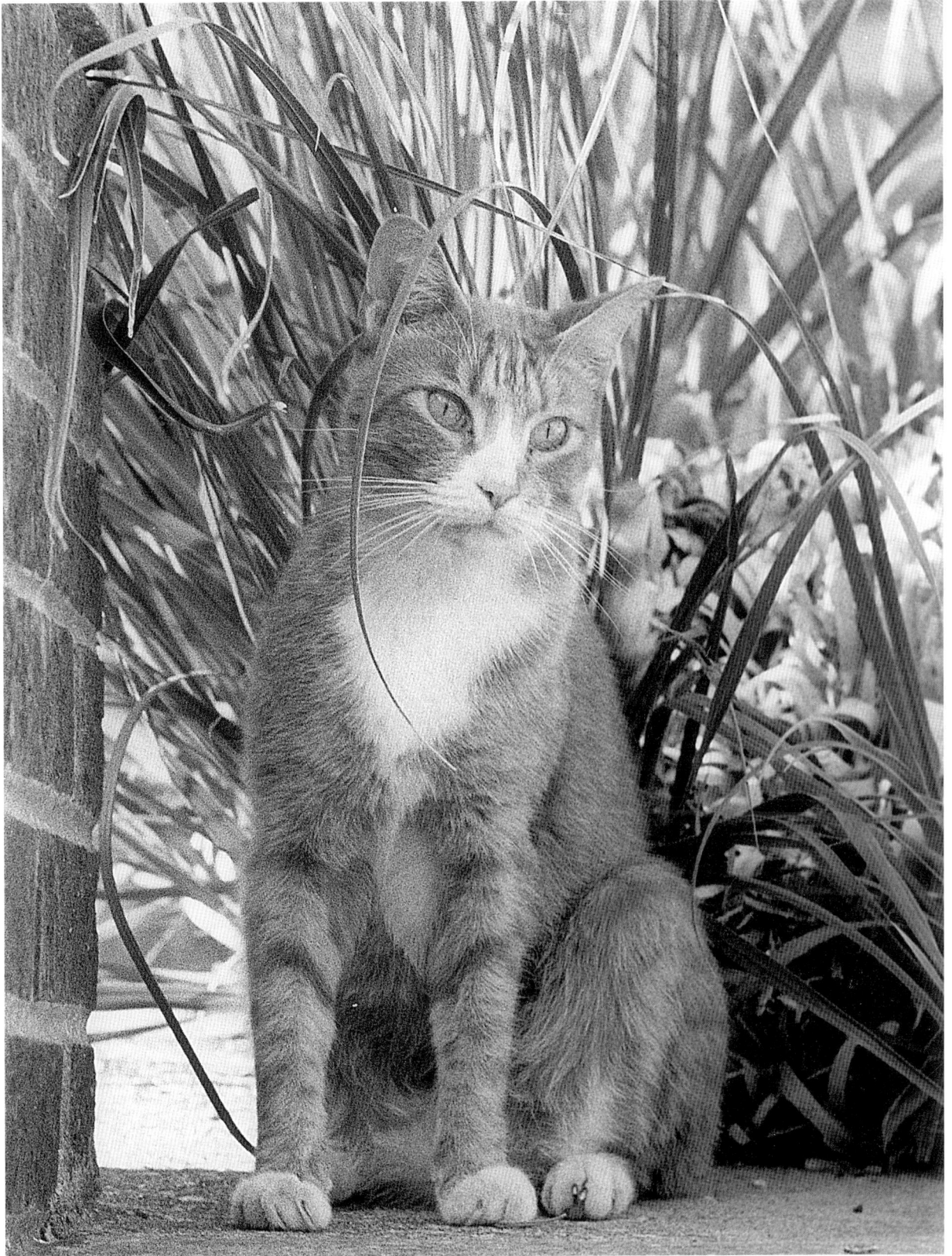

DOWN-MARKET

We're the boys from Sandown
And we don't think folks should hand down
Posh
Tosh.
It's just a lot of blather and
It's typical of Yaverland.
We're always on the move
And we'll prove
We're not yobs
Why, we've all got jobs.
It's hard to be forgiving
When we're working for a living
It's certainly not nice
When we're busy catching mice
Exhausted from our labours
To have insults from our neighbours
Hotels really need us
And occasionally feed us
Many an infested store
Near the shore
Are glad of our presence
We are the essence
Of rectitude
And good attitude
Though we agree
We may not have a pedigree
We rid the place of vermin
So we're worth our weight in ermine.

JAKE AWAKE

In Seaview's sweet tranquillity
My lissom limber loose-limbed cat
Sleeps supine in the sun
And you could shake him
Yet not wake him
Till his deep revitalising doze was done
He'll stretch a supple pliant paw
Then, snake-like arch and undulate
And sighing, slumber on.
Perhaps I ought to say
This happens at mid-day;
When midnight comes his indolence is gone
He'll jump about upon my bed
My lively heavy large-limbed cat
Like a drunken kangaroo
Who said "You can't disturb the cat"?
I can't agree with that
For what about the cat disturbing you?

TROY BOY

A cat called Troy
A black and white boy
Lived near Niton
Right on
The edge of the village
He'd pillage
Any food left unattended
Thus he offended
A few
Who never knew
He had no home
And had to roam
Unwelcomed until
In the evening chill
A boy
Befriended Troy
Then his family opted
To be kind, and adopted
This black and white loner.
He's now got an owner
His life was made
And there he stayed from that
Night on.

REBEL

They say
We're going away
I say
Were's away?
I heard
The word
Mainland
Is that the same land?
The Island's
My land
So much to-ing and fro-ing
Where are we going?
I see them stacking
Boxes, and packing
They say they're glad
I'm sad
Daily I meet
The cats down the street
The gardens I laze in
The windows I gaze in
Sounds that I know
I don't want to go
I won't leave Shide
I think I'll hide.

STARLET

You can't say she hasn't got glamour
The star of the felines in Brook
Marlena is lazy, is lovely and spoilt
With her languorous, sensuous look.

She doesn't go far promenading
As she hip-swings her way down the lane
The tilt of her head and her wink and her glance
Will sustain jealous views that she's vain.

But she once lost her elegant image
She escaped on the way to the vet
The locals were all quite astounded and shocked
When she crawled home bedraggled and wet.

It took her some time to recover
Her dignity, bearing and poise
But now she's regaining her chic and her style
And is once more attracting the boys.

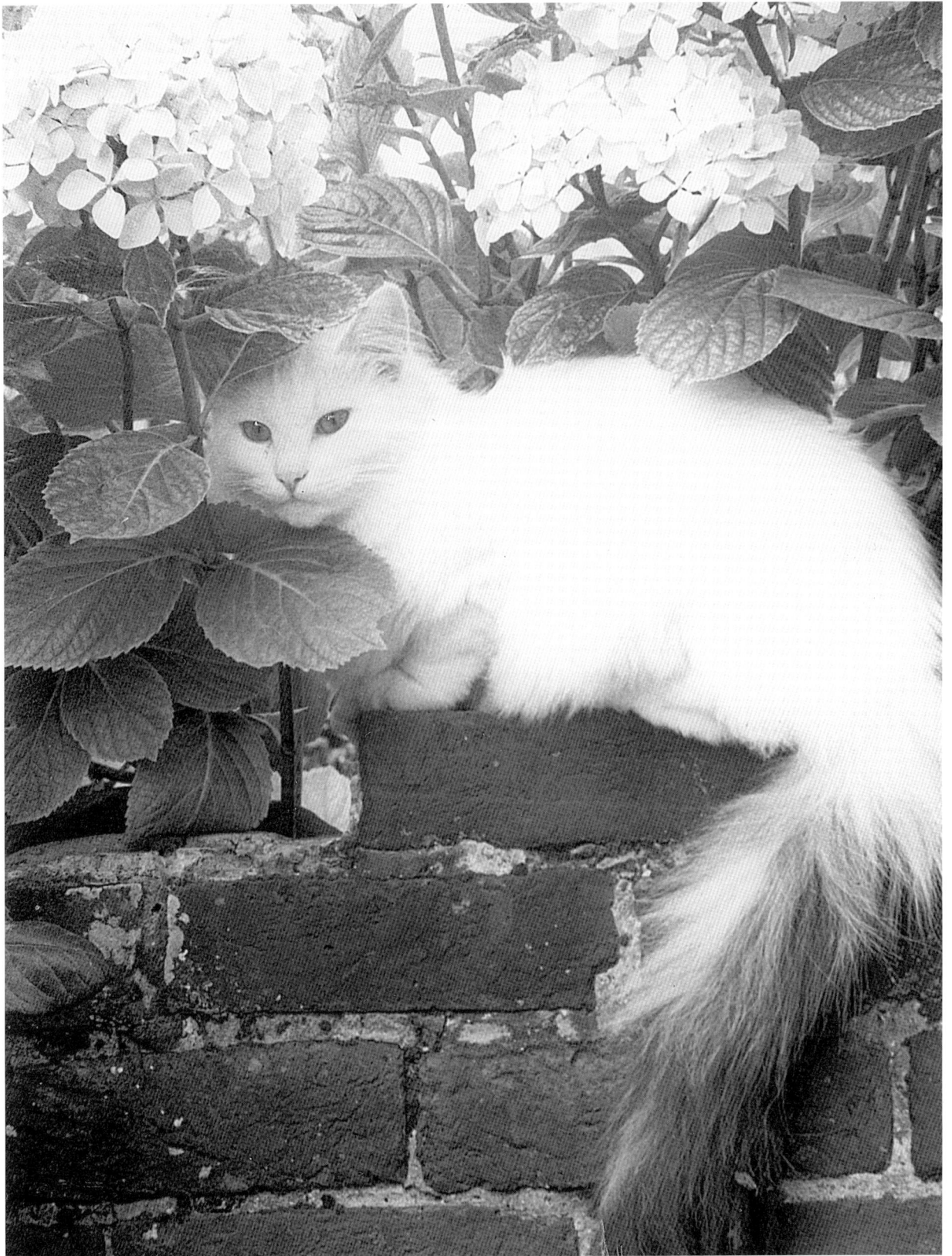

PICKED AND NICKED

I felt like aiding
That feline in Brading
The thinnest cat that you could ever find
Her meals were rare and frugal
As she searched around the Bugle
For scraps that well-fed diners left behind.
She raced across the road
Such recklessness she showed
My faith in her survival started fading
She ignored the fast approach
Of car and van and coach
Even caravans and bikes she was evading.
I decided to abduct
And gently to conduct
This black and skinny person to my home
She now has care in plenty
And food enough for twenty
And so I hope she'll never want to roam.
But she gives me such a fright
When she will go out at night
I wonder, is she looking for a pub?
Ah – there's the rub!

PARISHIONERS

Those two cats from Chale
Will not often fail
To behave in a dignified manner
With temptation they'll grapple
(They live in a Chapel)
And carry their tails like a banner

They're very aware
They have to take care
Not to make a mistake or a bloomer
And when in the house
They'll wink at a mouse
Who will think they've a great sense of humour.

They do love to roam
A long way from home
Where they're often outrageous and skittish
But their antics they'll quell
If they hear a church bell
And at once they're well-mannered and British.

DAREDEVIL

My cat who plays in the upstairs hall
Frightens us all
The bannister is his favourite walk
Tail upright he'll steadily stalk
I hold my breath
"He'll fall to his death"
I daily whisper
While he's a whisker
Away from a slip
While I take a grip
On my nerves
When he suddenly swerves
To turn on his paw
I'm watching with awe
How does he do it?
He's putting me through it
Should I offer my pet
A small safety net?
He's not very tiny
And my bannister's shiny
I don't like to call
He'd probably fall
D'you know the relief that I feel
When my Benjie comes down for a meal?

Uptails All

Who will free me from this spraying beast
Who, when the springtime instincts call
Avails himself of ev'ry budding bush
Non-stop, and right into the hall?

It isn't that he hasn't been "arranged"
His brother too has seen the vet
But <u>he</u> is circumspect – restrains his tail
From flying up – he's not a jet-set pet

Our menace obviously feels he must
Earmark his territory claims
Except it's not his ear which is at fault
And he is not too fussy where he aims

When guests are due to visit us at Lake
We rush around and mop the floor
While burning joss-sticks – smile – apologise,
And blame "that awful cat next door"

Upstairs Cat

Seal sleek my sheer jet pet
Nightly seeks the stairs
Then up she'll run
The only one
To share my room
The other felines sleep downstalrs
She never cares
To share their lives
At night she thrives
And that is when
She then becomes
A different kind of cat.
Night begins with chitter chatter
And no matter
If I understand or not – she's got a way
To quite convey
Her meaning
After all the conversation
Sheer elation takes its place
The pace accelerates
She'll see a cobweb on the wall
I see her leap – feel sure she'll fall
Jut then she's rounding up
The catnip mouse the fluffy ball
And all she wants is noisy play
Yet come the day
She's quite withdrawn
A yawn is all you'll get
From my black pet
Downstairs the daytime
Ends her playtime
We're aware
She doesn't care
For the boys who stay down there.

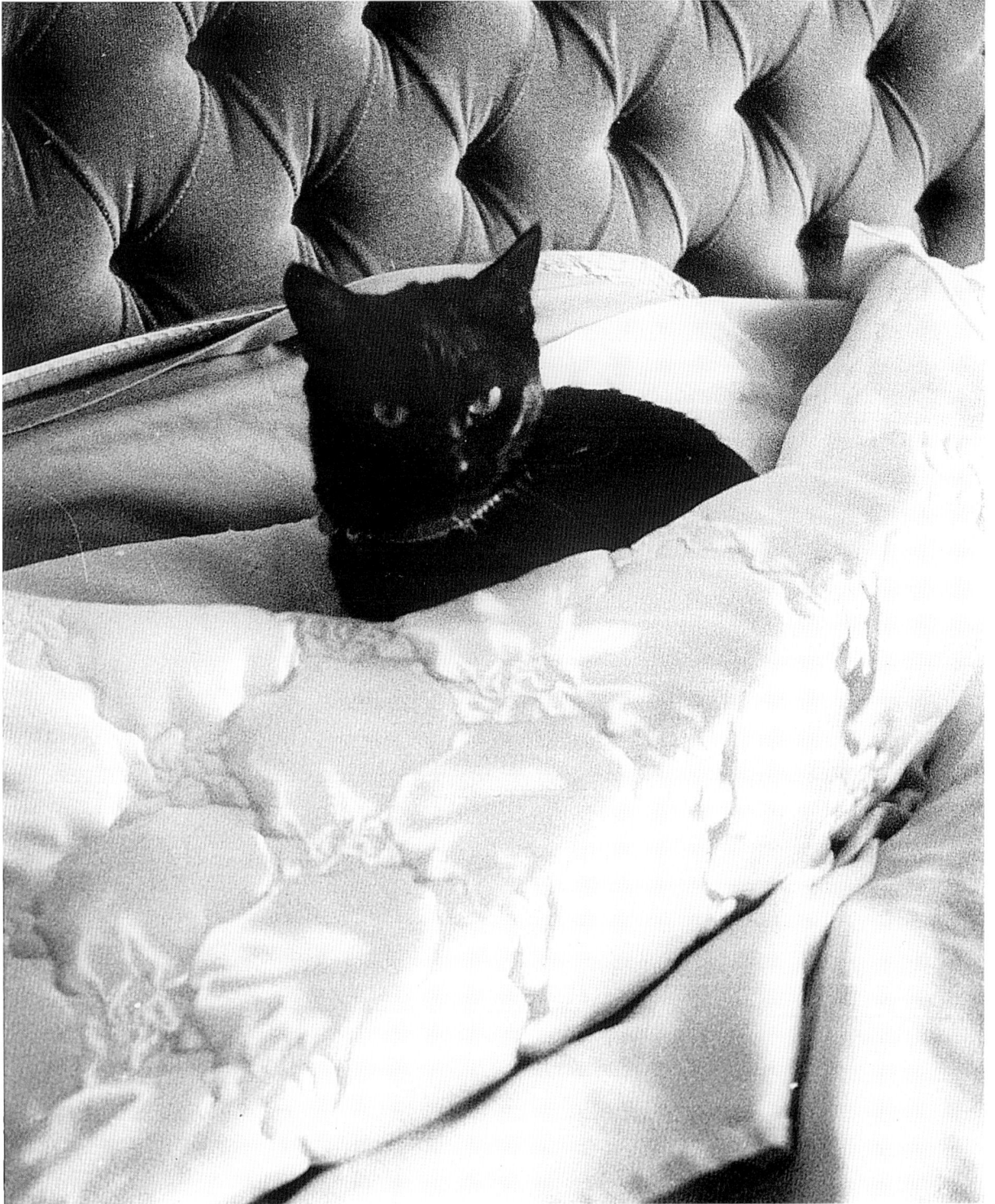

CAT SITTER

It's simply a fluke
That we came across Luke
In a Ryde convenience store
I asked – was he resident – did he belong?
I looked at the girl, I could see I was wrong
No cat-lover she, I was sure.
The shop-girl retorted "Ten times I've escorted
That cat to the door – and I shout!
But he keeps coming back
They'll give me the sack
If I can't keep that animal out

My neighbour is fond
And has a great bond
With cats who've had much to endure
And Luke had most carelessly lost half a tail
His fur was unkempt and his nose very pale –
So he soon was adopted next door
His looks have improved
And I felt myself moved
To photograph him on the fence
And though not offended
At once he descended
And showed his artistic good sense.

I think that he knew
The work that I do
He'd seen photos around I suppose
He'd noticed my studio, such a bright place
He came in the door with a purr on his face
And struck quite an elegant pose.
We worked on that sitting
I don't mind admitting
I bribed him with many a snack
Of nice bits of food
(It's something I've rued)
For Luke can't resist coming back.

Weighty Problem

It isn't that Tubs is greedy
He's just got a good appetite
He has his main meal in the morning
And another main meal at night.

Tubs does like a top-up at lunch time
And a rather big meal for his tea
And of course he needs biscuits between times
And any odd snack he can see.

Cowes neighbours will often give titbits
Although they agree he's quite stout
He can't enter anyone's cat-flap
For he's captured, half in and half out.

He once was put on a diet
It gave him much grief and much pain
His looks gave his owners a conscience
So he's back to full banquets again.

UPROAR

Why don't you get on?
You'd both seen hard times
Long before you met me
I hoped that there'd be
A strong fellow feeling
For troubles you'd known
Of being alone
Not knowing just when you'd next eat
The street
Was your home, your refuge and larder
A harder
Environment than you have here
With Newchurch so near
So quiet and peaceful and bright
Yet you fight
You've both been invited to share
My table, my bed and my very best chair
I care
For your needs, so I think I'm deserving
Unswerving
Regard for my books and my curtains
And any odd treasure
Your pleasure is just to annoy
And destroy as much as you can
Your plan
For the end of the day is a fight
At night
I decide I should simply just send you away
Comes the day
Then I say
Don't stray – please stay
For you know that's the way
You become when you've cats

Lap-cat

This lady in Totland works very hard
And she's got a favourite armchair
But when work is finished – she wants to relax
She finds Phoebe her cat sitting there

There are times when she's weary and sleepy
And ready to go to her bed
Lying crosswise and fully spread out
Her Phoebe is lodged there instead

She once bought a beautiful hammock
For her garden for days in the sun
She's never been able to use it herself
For her cat thinks it wonderful fun

She once had a very nice boy friend
An affectionate good-looking chap
But when she approached in the hope of a cuddle
There was Phoebe, ensconced on his lap

It isn't that she ever gets in a rage
For she loves her to utter distraction
That's why when when she steals all her favourite things
She is spurred – to total inaction.

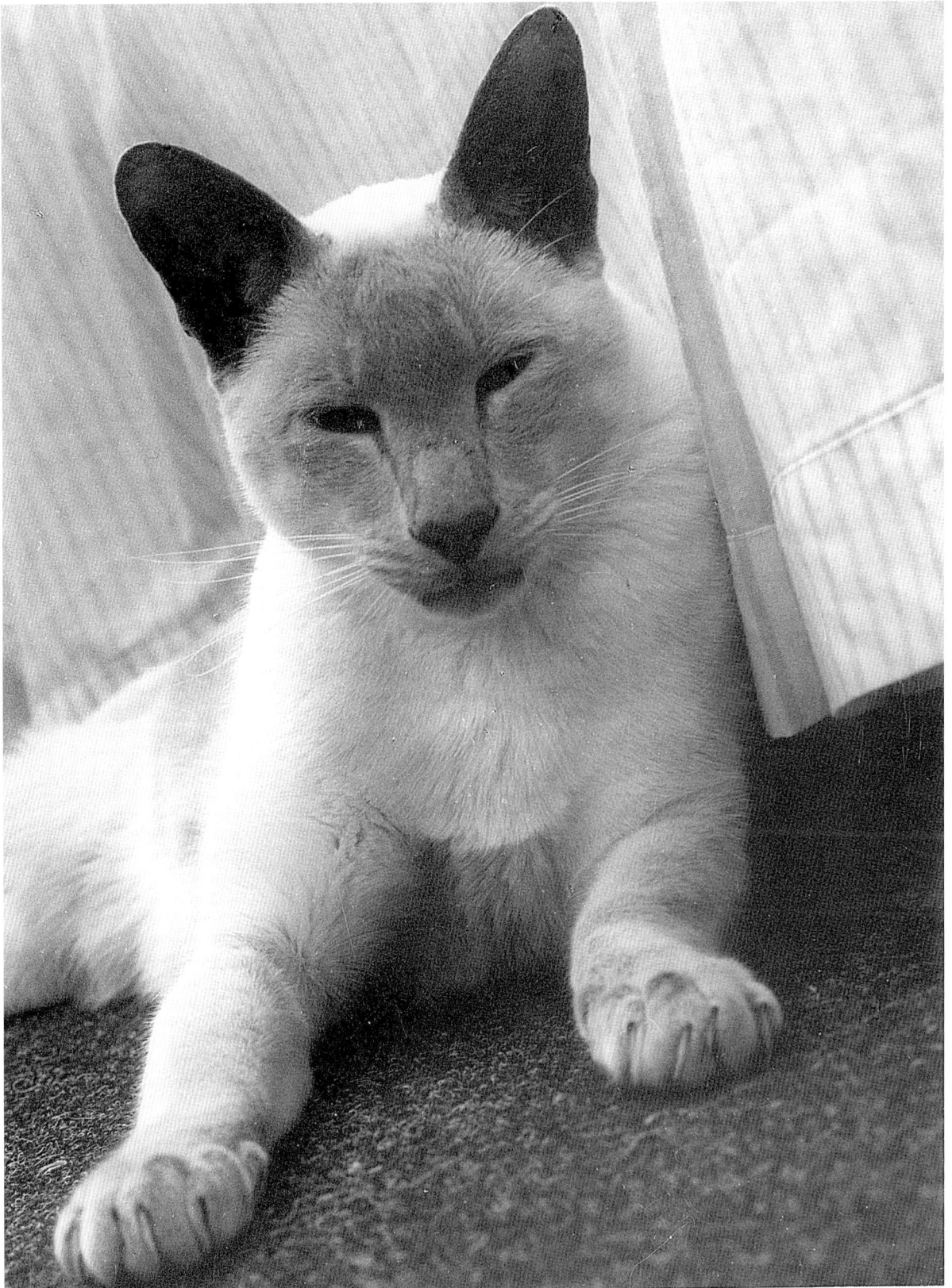

MANX

I once met a Manx on the banks of the Yar
How he arrived there nobody knows
Did he walk did he run did he fly and how far?
Did he swim, I thought with a shudder
For he'd got no tail as a rudder

It's sad for the Manx with his flanks trimmed and bare
What is his suffering – nobody knows
His whole silhouette tends to look a bit square
When he's cross then his pride he must pick up
For he hasn't a tail he can flick up

I now rate the Manx with the ranks of the brave
Why deprivation? Nobody knows
His character's strong but his manner is grave
If he's happy you might think he's flagging
He's got no appendage for wagging

But this little pet who's known as a Manx
Is loving and loyal as everyone knows
He will purr he will play he will get up to pranks
When he's saucy, though missing his whatnot
He will just waggle what he has not got.

CLAWS AND EFFECT

We called him "Nipper" Dave from Ryde said
Just because he was so small
Such a friendly purring creature
Dearly loved by one and all

Just sit down and soon he'll greet you
Quickly on your lap he'll land
Stroke him fondly soon you'll find he'll
Swiftly turn and nip your hand

All his family make excuses
"He's a loving playfellow –
Sorry he's a touch neurotic
Love endures – and wounds will go"

Dave's got hands criss-crossed with scratches
From the creature that he loves
Says "You'd like to cuddle Nipper?"
"Take these hefty leather gloves"

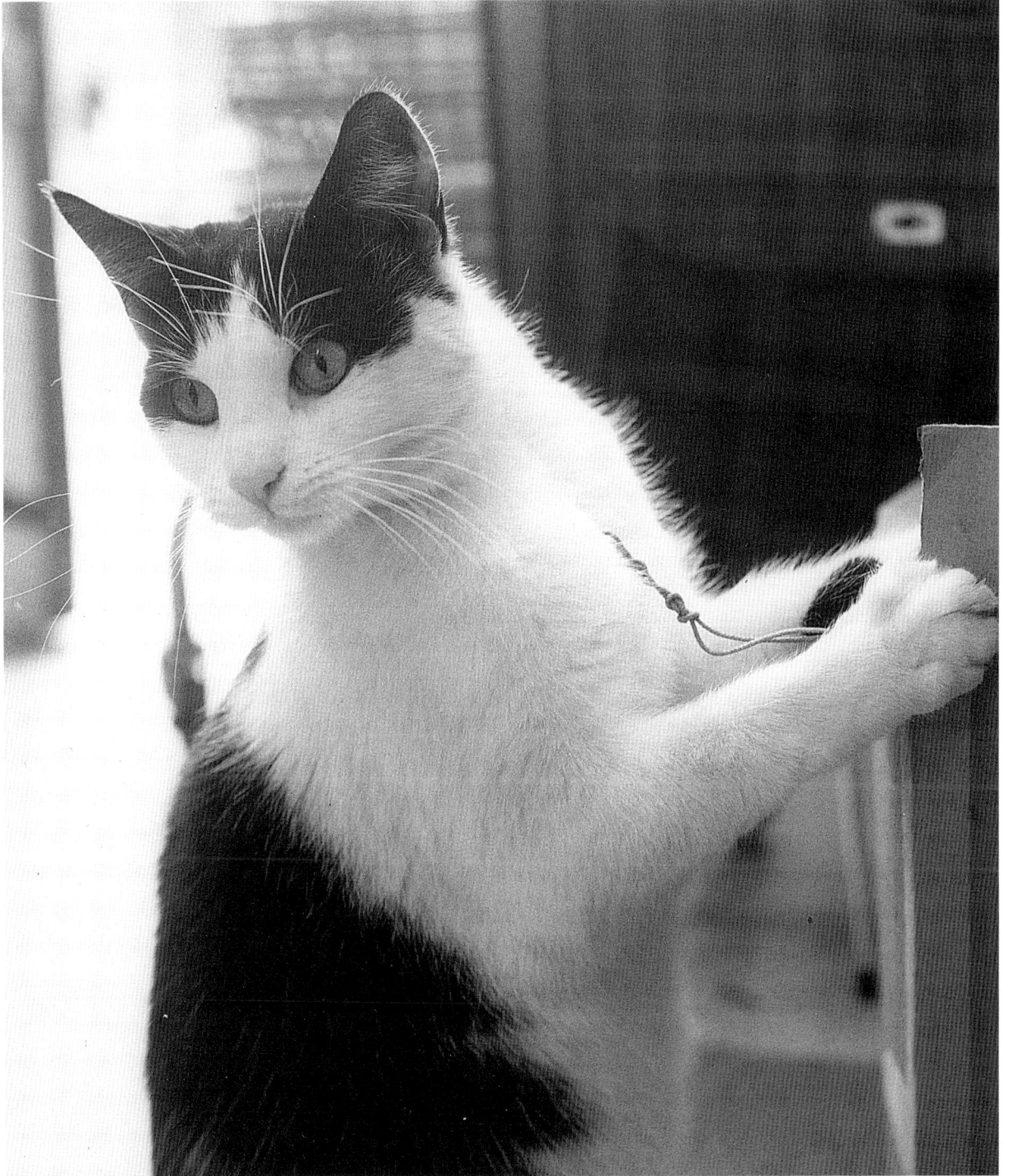

SENIOR CITIZEN

Magnus is an elder
Of the cat fraternity
He knows the pedigree
Of all the cats in his locality
Cat of mystery
He knows the history
Of this Island nation
Each cat generation
Passing on the stories
Of ancient glories
Fighting a French invasion –
Occupation
By Roman legions
Many regions
Of this island crowned with villas
Pillars
Everywhere
For cats to hide behind
(When so inclined)
Poets, artists, writers fascinated
By this Isle
Have stayed a while.
But Magnus knows
That while much comes and goes
Cats ways remain immutable
And they are of course Inscrutable.

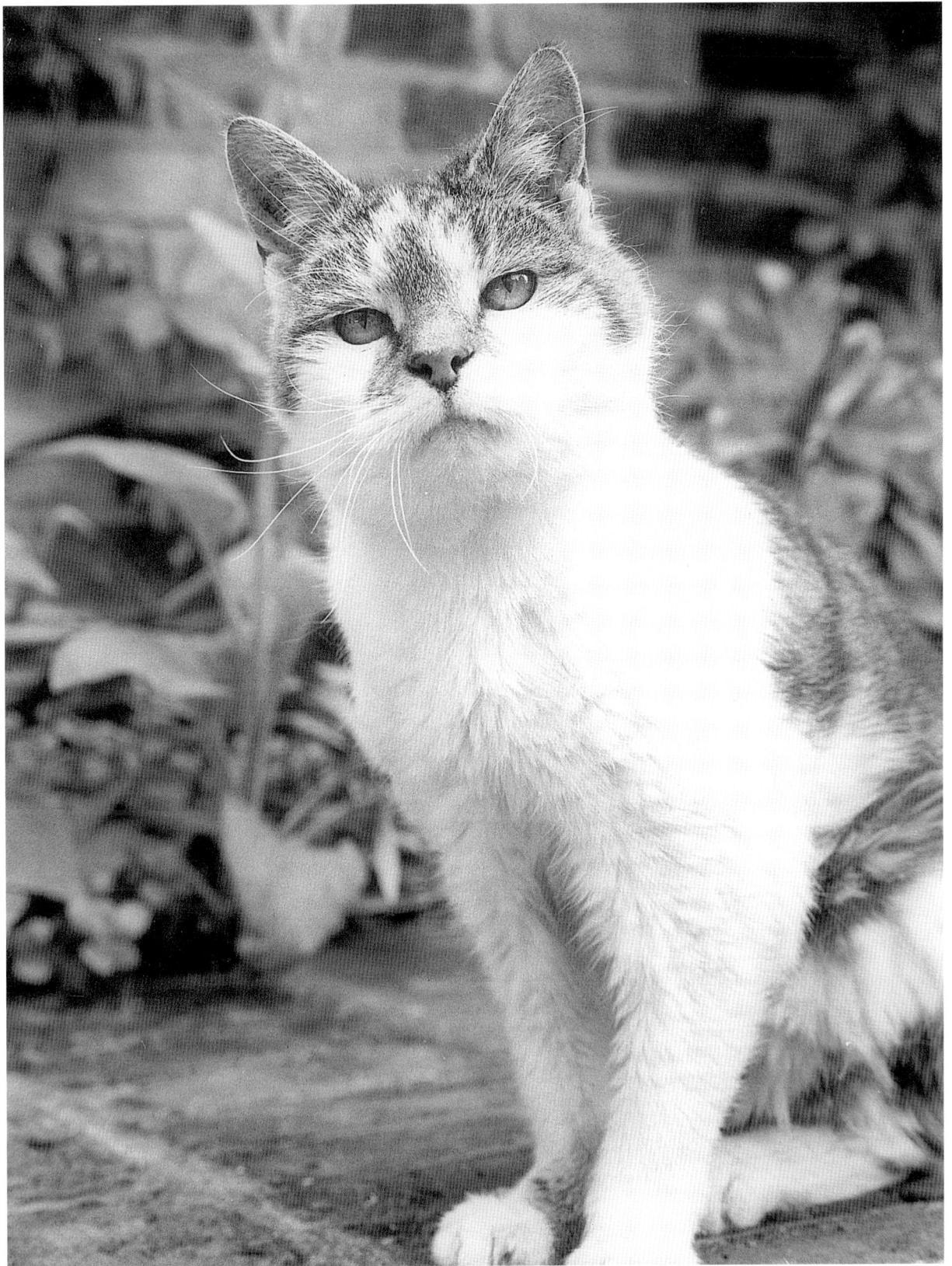

ADGESTONE DREAMER

The sky is still blue, yet see the leaves falling,
Showering all over my place in the sun
The flowers are all gone and the warmth is now fading
I'm a cat and I know a new season's begun.

The birds all above me fly higher and higher,
The whirr of their wings match the wind in the trees
Upstream and downstream a million dark feathers
Where do they go – crossing land crossing seas.

I am a cat and my climbing is graceful
High up on fences or trees a mile high
I see the horizon, the birds disappearing
And yet I can't fly, oh why can't I fly?

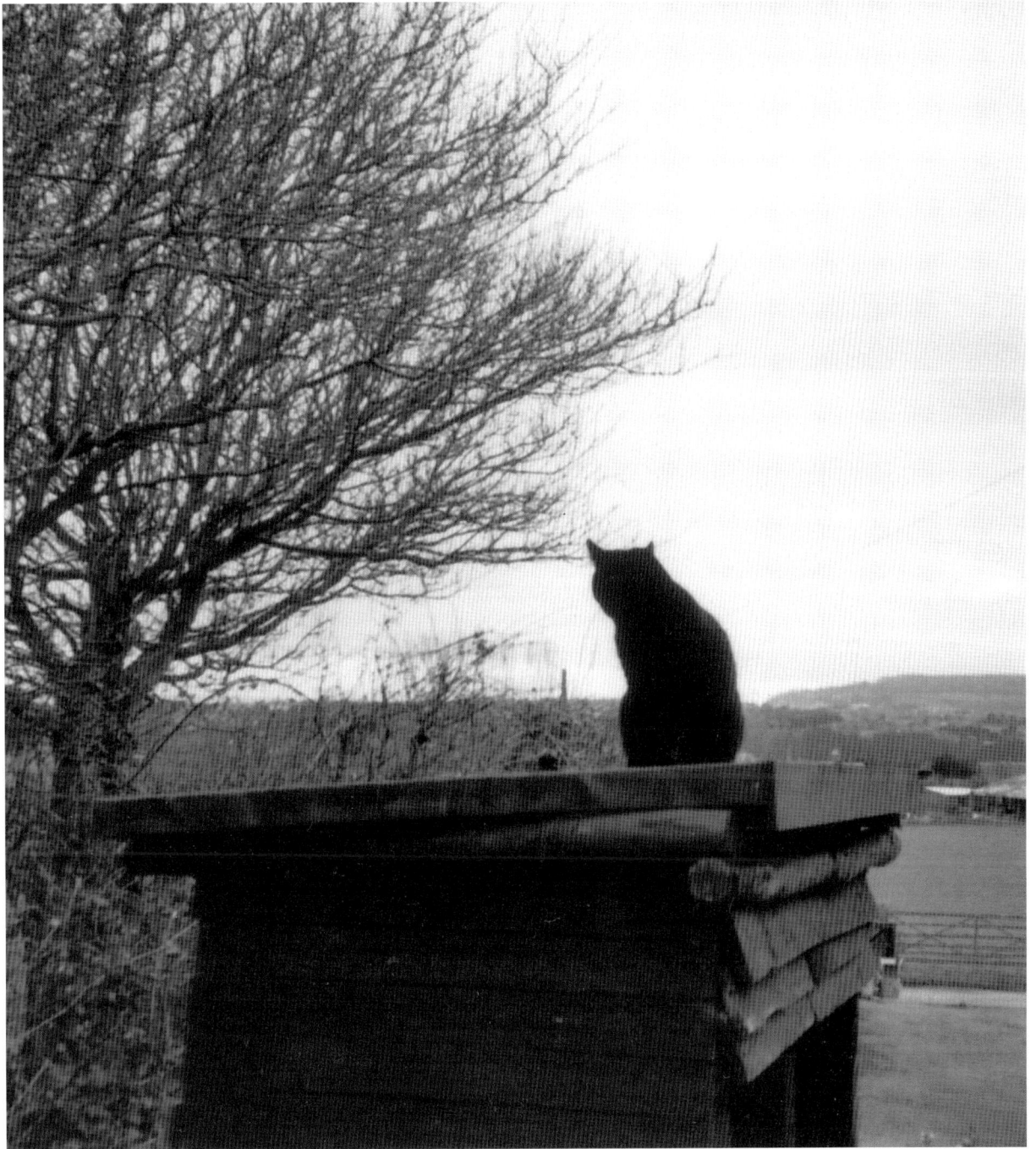

Billie Love has had a fascinating and interesting career. Born into a theatrical family she herself played leading parts in the West End of London for many years. Then she branched out into photography and had various studios in Central London. Concurrent with this Billie ran her own historical Picture Library.

Shortly after moving to the Isle of Wight in 1989 she went into publishing, the first being a book of poems about cats, called 'Opusses' and the second called 'How to become a Child', combining historical photographs and her humourous philosophy about children. This, her third book is verse and pictures about the feline characters of the Island.

Many of Billie Loves verses and photographs have been published in *The Lady* magazine.

Anna Shepherd